Table of Contents

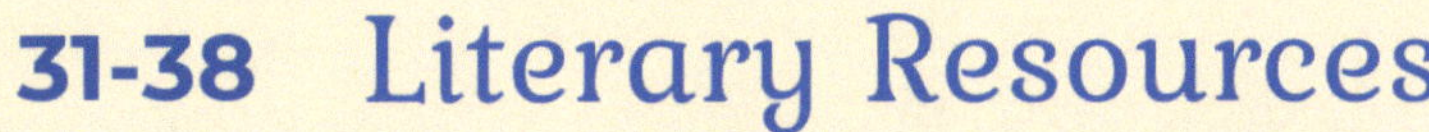

Paulette Henson
Editor's Note

Dear Readers,

Celebrating the Essence of Black Womanhood: A Journey Through Words
In the vibrant tapestry of literature, Black women authors have woven threads of resilience, wisdom, and beauty, crafting narratives that illuminate the rich tapestry of their experiences. BWA Magazine proudly celebrates the profound impact of Black women authors, whose voices resonate across generations, continents, and cultures.

Empowering Narratives: Black women authors stand at the forefront of literary excellence, fearlessly exploring themes of identity, heritage, and empowerment. Their stories delve deep into the complexities of life, offering insights, inspiration, and hope to readers worldwide. From powerful memoirs to captivating fiction, each page of BWA Magazine is adorned with the brilliance of their storytelling.

Unveiling Untold Stories: Within the pages of BWA Magazine, hidden histories are unearthed, and silenced voices are amplified. Black women authors courageously confront societal injustices, challenge stereotypes, and reclaim their narratives with unwavering determination. Their words serve as beacons of truth, illuminating the path towards a more inclusive and equitable world.

A Platform for Expression: BWA Magazine provides a platform for Black women authors to share their stories, celebrate their achievements, and connect with a diverse audience of readers. Through thought-provoking interviews, insightful essays, and captivating book features, BWA Magazine honors the brilliance and resilience of Black women in literature.

Inspiring Future Generations: As torchbearers of literary excellence, Black women authors inspire future generations to dream, create, and thrive. Their words serve as catalysts for change, sparking conversations, and igniting movements for social justice and equality. BWA Magazine is dedicated to uplifting and empowering the voices of Black women authors, ensuring that their legacies endure for generations to come.

Join the Celebration: Embark on a literary journey like no other with BWA Magazine. Discover the diverse voices, powerful stories, and transformative wisdom of Black women authors who continue to shape the landscape of literature. With each issue, BWA Magazine celebrates the essence of Black womanhood and honors the enduring legacy of Black women in literature.

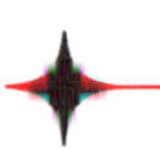

Author April Mack Wilson

"Bold Enough" is a powerful book that aims to empower individuals to lead lives that honor their calling. It encompasses God's faith, hope, and inspiration to persevere through difficult times.

Through authentic and heartfelt conversations, April shares her journey through vulnerable moments, addressing experiences with hurt, depression and PTSD, anxiety, inadequacy, and the weight of burdens carried alone. As a woman of faith, she emphasizes the importance of leaning on God's Word and way and encourages readers to do the same.

The unique journal-style conversations, inspiring devotionals, and journal prompts within the book offer words of encouragement and hope. They remind us that no one is alone in life's trials and that victory awaits on the other side. Her words provide the motivation and support needed

Available on Amazon
HTTPS://A.CO/D/1YOSPRB

to stand strong amidst daily challenges and to foster a deeper connection with God. April, an Air Force Veteran who served in Afghanistan and a registered nurse who endured the COVID-19 pandemic, knows firsthand what it looks like to emerge refined and perfected by God after enduring life's battles. She wants you to embark on the daily journey to be "Bold Enough" and walk into everything God predestined for you. You are an overcomer, and God wants to use you in His Kingdom. He is the God of second chances, and it is never too late to live in the

purpose and promises of your Father.

Author
Tiffany Flowers Towns

Tiffany Flowers Towns has always enjoyed writing. Her work includes poems, short stories, songs, and her first novella, I Wish I Had Never... and the sequel I Thought I Would Never... as well as a children's book Amiyah and Jaxon Learn the Power of "YET"! and a women's devotional, The Master's Pieces: 30 Intimate Devotionals from Women in the Word. She is also an avid reader and enjoys singing. Tiffany is a graduate of the University of North Florida, where she earned her Bachelor's degree in Elementary Education and her Master's degree in Educational Leadership. As a lifelong educator and administrator, she is not only doing what she loves, but she is inspiring the next generation to do the same. She is a Christian who loves the Lord. Tiffany is also a proud member of Delta Sigma Theta Sorority, Incorporated. She resides in Jacksonville, Florida with her husband, Vince, and their two daughters, Crystal and Camryn.

Author

Dr. Gracie Kearse-McCastler

My name is Gracie Bell Kearse-McCastler. I am a retired teacher/assistant principal, minister, author, and community leader. My organization affiliations are Delta Sigma Theta Sorority, Incorporated, Bethel Baptist Church, Black Women Educational Leaders, and Black Women Authors.

As an educator, I taught for 33 years in primary education, grades K-2, and upon retirement became an assistant principal. My greatest accomplishments are attaining an AA degree, BA degree, MS degree, and a Doctoral degree.

As a minister, I have ministered for over 30 years and taught Sunday school for about 22 years. Presently, I am a minister for Delta Sigma Theta Sorority, Incorporated. My first Christian book is Reconnecting with the Forgotten Fruit.

As an author, the four published books are Transforming Into An Effective Leader, Lead by Example, Transforming Truancy and Reconnecting with the Forgotten Fruit. Also, I am a published poet. Writing is a hobby of mine and I love expressing myself with the written word.

As a community leader, using my political knowledge, experiences, and influence is another hat worn by me. I have served on various committees with the City Hall. Presently, I am serving on several committees with the U.S. White House. I am a voice in the community for the political issues, educational issues, elderly, youth and the disenfranchised. Social Action is what I do, as well.
Dr. Gracie Bell Kearse-McCastler

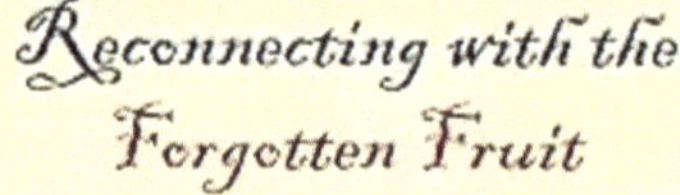

Dating Like A Football Coach —Finding Your MVP
By
Stephanie Bailey

Dating can be similar to a football coach who's recruiting the best player for his team. When I was dating prior to meeting my partner I dating multiple men until I found a connection that I could envision longterm.

Dating like a football coach—for my sports ladies and not sports ladies.

The football player (man you are dating) will get the coach (you) to the playoffs (commitment) after proving (with his actions) that he is serious about you—bringing the coach (you) the *Super Bowl Ring* (engagement ring).

Depending on how many men you are recruiting (dating) at one time, there will be some fumbles (with the men you date) —leaving one (or a few men) on the field (in your life)—these are the guys who are making touchdowns/field goals (genuine effort)—possibly winning your heart. Some men will eventually get pulled from the game and benched (the effort is lacking) due to incompletions, fumbles or interceptions (your interest is fading). And, there will be those who have completely given you the ick (personal foul) and are permanently sent to the locker room (no longer a top draft pick), or worse—demoted to water boy.

If he's not connecting with you emotionally to make you want him (high percent of his passes are incomplete), the effort to see you is lacking (fumbling on his runs), and wooing you/taking you on dates lessens (doesn't make the first down)—it might be time to let him go.

The beautiful thing about being the coach of your own dating life is that you decide who you want to date, when you are free for the date and how often each guy will get to see you. Dating more than one guy gives you options which can help you figure out what you really want— especially if you don't know already. Dating like a football coach will help you differentiate the guys who are truly interested from the ones who are just playing "the game." The guy who makes the effort to look at his schedule in advance, plans time to see you, will essentially be the one to be your Starter (win your heart).

Just like in football, to be the best player is similar to what woman look for and (deep down) want in a guy. Ladies here are some great qualities to look for when recruiting your team and eventually your ultimate quarterback (love of your life).

To Make A Great Football Player (dater/potential boyfriend), this is the advice I give men:

1. Know that you can achieve your goal: In dating terms—be confident, not cocky.

2. Be in great shape: We're not asking for perfect, however most woman want a man who takes care of himself. Eating healthy and working out helps us visualize a future, in which you will be around and active.

3. Practice the basics of football: Don't be a lazy dater—make an effort—we like to feel special and appreciated.

4. Find a position you like to play: We aren't attracted to men who tell us they are one way — understanding, open-minded, respectful, and later devalue us, get an attitude quickly, or display inappropriate anger. We prefer men whose actions speak louder than words—not the other way around (we don't want to guess if we are dating Prince Charming or Dr. Jekyll/Mr. Hyde)

5. Practice the skills for your position: We love men who are passionate: knowing what your language of love is and using it to make that connection (the right woman will appreciate it).

6. Be aware of your competition: If you know we are dating other men, don't lack in your efforts (if you possibly can see a future in us), step up your game—competition goes away when the the best man is making the effort.

7. Be tough and secure: We prefer a man who is strong. Strong enough to know when he's wrong. Strong enough to back down and not start a fight—but will fight to keep us in their life. Strong enough to be by our side. Strong enough to be vulnerable. Strong enough to not be afraid of love and commitment.

8. Get along with your team members: It's important to us that our friends and family like you and that you have a supportive group of friends and family who also like us.

9. Get ready to win: Again, if you are confident and know that you want to be with us—we will feel it too, and eventually choose you.

10. Understand that anything less than your absolute maximum 100% effort on every play (date) is a recipe for mediocrity, if you want to be our MVP (our boyfriend), you must attack every play (moment with us) with all your physical (chemistry and passion) and mental (your personality) skills operating at their absolute maximum: This is my favorite and says it all!

11. When you're off the field, listen to the coaches or coordinators: If you want a successful relationship than don't get advice from your single forever bachelor friends, talk to your friends who are in great relationships. Talk to a therapist to help open your heart and trust in love again. Talk to supportive family members. Read inspiring self-help books. Do what ever works for you to make the relationship last.

Dating like a football coach can be fun—who doesn't like to have choices when you're single? Playing the field can be a great way for helping you figure out what you want, and finding the best match for you.

Ladies, if you are in the the dating field, but are open to the possibilities of a relationship—it's important to be honest and let the men know who you are dating, so that they don't feel as if you are just a player or a tease. Take adequate time, but not an unreasonable, selfish amount or time, to figure out who your star player is, before another woman recruits him before you. Learn the dating skills of downsizing, make adjustments and follow your heart, not your loins. If you are lucky you will find a man who will stay in the game and win the *Super Bowl* of your heart.

MISS-ADVENTURES LOVE COACHING
EMPOWERING WOMEN ON ALL ASPECTS OF LOVE

Stephanie is a Certified Master Life Coach, the CEO of Miss-Adventures, LLC, three-time #1 Bestselling author, and #1 New Release. Stephanie's mission is empowering women on all aspects of love. She strongly believes in the power of prayer and affirmations to ignite and create the love, health, wealth, success, family, abundance, relationships, and prosperity we want in our lives. Stephanie is a podcaster, public speaker, published writer—over 250 articles between hubpages, Paired Life and Elephant Journal. She has also been a guest on multiple radio and podcast shows. Stephanie has been mentoring women for over 26-plus years and offers in-person and virtual sessions.

STEPHANIE BAILEY

BENEFITS OF SELF-LOVE:

- Personal Growth
- Using your voice—not being afraid to speak up.
- Confronting your fears.
- Empowering yourself through forgiveness—to release being a victim.
- And more…

"Stephanie is an exceptionally valuable expert on relationship advice. Over the years her wisdom and guidance have been at the core of my personal growth on my journey. xoxoxo Love you!"

— NANCY G., COLORADO

CONTACT:

323-332-9976
MISS-ADVENTURES.COM

MISS-ADVENTURES.COM

Doris Pinkett "Pinke Loved"

Presidential Lifetime Achievement Award Recipient, and Self-Published Author of "REFRESHED: A Journey of Reflections and Connections", Doris Pinkett is the founder of The Pinke Loved Institute, a platform designed to uplift women, particularly divorced women as they engage into new experiences and reset their lives after divorce. Doris jumped into the world of writing a few years after her 16-year marriage shockingly ended due to a $500 disagreement. The growth and revelations she experienced are penned inside this book. This Women's Empowerment Speaker has a sincere desire to uplift and celebrate women, as they make a comeback, and excel in every area of their lives. A native of Atlanta, Georgia, and a graduate of the Tennessee State University, Doris is the proud mother of 3 adult children, Nemiah (24), Melaiah (22) and JaH'son (21), all of whom are pursuing college degrees, and are leaders in their own right. Whether it be through her speaking, writing or her "REFRESHED" Yoga series, she aspires to engage, elevate, encourage, enlighten and empower women so they can maximize their purpose, both personally and professionally.

****
20/20 Enterprises Certified Speaker
Breathe for Change Certified Yoga and SEL Facilitator
2023 Sisterhood-On-The-Go Community Service Award Recipient

For Bookings and Inquiries:
Phone Number: 404-207-7212
Website: https://linktr.ee/Pinkeloved
Facebook: Pinke Loved
Instagram: pinkelovedinstitute
Email: pinkelovedllc@gmail.com

✦ AUTHOR
Nia Hunt

Nia Hunt's story is one of resilience and triumph in the face of adversity. Born and raised on the streets of Philadelphia, Nia experienced a tough childhood, with her parents abandoning her as a toddler and leaving her to face the world alone. As a result, Nia was placed in foster care, where she had to navigate through various trials and tribulations that left her feeling helpless and heartbroken.

Despite her challenges, Nia found solace and comfort in writing poetry, which allowed her to express her pain and connect with her inner self and others. Over time, Nia's passion for writing grew. She pursued her education with unwavering determination, earning an associate degree in web/graphic designing and a bachelor's in criminal justice. Her academic achievements are a testament to her commitment to personal growth and overcoming adversity. She is currently working towards a master's in law, further demonstrating her resilience and dedication.

Today, Nia is living her dream of being a successful poet, published author, songwriter, and business owner. Her personal experiences, especially her time in foster care, have deeply influenced her work. She has recently published her first book, "Being Intentional Journal-Purpose Driven," Which reflects her journey toward healing and self-discovery. She has created her own company, Intentional Sentiments, which specializes in a unique greeting card collection and other products designed to inspire and bring joy.

WITH EVERY CARD, BOOK, AND PRODUCT SOLD BY INTENTIONAL SENTIMENTS, NIA'S VISION AND PASSION FOR REACHING, COMFORTING, HEALING, AND LOVING INTENTIONALLY SHINES THROUGH, MAKING A TANGIBLE DIFFERENCE IN THE LIVES OF HER CUSTOMERS AND THE COMMUNITY.

INTENTIONAL SENTIMENTS BELIEVES IN DELIBERATELY SPREADING UNCONDITIONAL LOVE, AS STATED IN 1 CORINTHIANS 13:13: "AND NOW THERE REMAIN FAITH [ABIDING IN GOD AND HIS PROMISES], HOPE [CONFIDENT EXPECTATION OF ETERNAL SALVATION], LOVE [UNSELFISH LOVE FOR OTHERS GROWING OUT OF GOD'S LOVE FOR ME], THESE THREE [THE CHOICEST GRACES]; BUT THE GREATEST OF THESE IS LOVE." THROUGH HER COMPANY, NIA IS MAKING A DIFFERENCE IN THE WORLD BY SPREADING LOVE AND INSPIRATION AND PLANTING SEEDS OF HOPE. IN THE FUTURE, NIA HOPES TO EXPAND HER COMPANY'S REACH AND IMPACT, AND CONTINUE TO USE HER VOICE AND CREATIVITY TO INSPIRE OTHERS.

LEGACY
A Novel by Cheryl Garrison

Legacy by Cheryl Garrison is a poignant and compelling novel that delves into the intricate dynamics of a modern African American family while uncovering the dark and painful legacies of slavery. The story revolves around Marriah, Liz, and Nate, Jr., the children of Anna Howard, who has recently passed away. As they navigate the emotionally charged task of packing up their childhood home in Phoenix, they stumble upon an old leather-bound journal.

This discovery sets off a series of revelations that deeply impact the siblings. The journal, with its timeworn pages, reveals a harrowing secret intertwined with their family's history. Among its contents is an old photograph that particularly disturbs one of the sisters, forcing her to confront personal demons.

As the siblings delve deeper into the journal, they uncover brutal truths about their ancestors' involvement in slavery, including acts of murder. This painful history shakes the very foundation of their identity, bringing to light the often unspoken atrocities of the past.

The journey through the journal's revelations is transformative for the siblings. It compels them to face various personal and familial issues such as sibling rivalry, alcoholism, infidelity, and other hidden secrets that have long simmered beneath the surface.

About the Author

Cheryl Garrisonis the CEO of 50Something Lifestyle, a resource, coaching and publishing business for women over 50. She started Becoming 50Something Publications, a publishing wing of her business, to help women over 50 tell their story in a safe and affordable place. She is the author of seven nonfiction books for women over 50 who want to live their BEST life, right now!

Legacy is her first fiction book. For many years, Cheryl has been fascinated with the history of African Americans in this country, from slavery to present-day. She believes that African American families are all shaped by the roots of their ancestors, many of them who were slaves. Most fascinating to Cheryl are the slaves who were able to escape to freedom to a better life of freedom. Legacy is a culmination of Cheryl's passion for history and the legacy of family!

NOW AVAILABLE
https://www.50somethinglifestyle.com/new-releases

Author
Elizabeth Michaud

A Step-by-Step Guide to Writing Your Book

Writing a book is a journey of self-discovery, creativity, and perseverance. Whether you're an aspiring author with a story burning inside you or a seasoned writer looking to embark on your next literary adventure, the process of bringing your ideas to life can be both exhilarating and daunting. In this guide, we'll explore the essential steps to help you navigate the path from inspiration to publication and craft your masterpiece with confidence.

Step 1: Define Your Vision

Every great book begins with a clear vision. Take the time to define your goals, objectives, and the message you want to convey through your writing. Ask yourself: What story do I want to tell? Who is my target audience? What impact do I hope to make with my book? By clarifying your vision upfront, you'll lay a solid foundation for your writing journey.

Step 2: Develop Your Concept

Once you have a clear vision in mind, it's time to develop your concept and outline the structure of your book. Brainstorm ideas, themes, and plot points, and organize them into a cohesive framework. Whether you prefer a detailed outline or a more flexible approach, having a roadmap will guide your writing process and keep you focused as you flesh out your ideas.

Step 3: Commit to a Writing Routine

The key to making progress on your book is consistency. Set aside dedicated time each day or week to focus on your writing, and stick to your schedule religiously. Whether you're a morning person who thrives on early writing sessions or a night owl who prefers burning the midnight oil, find a routine that works for you and make writing a non-negotiable part of your daily life.

CRAFTING YOUR MASTERPIECE

Step 4: Write with Abandon
Writing the first draft of your book is a liberating experience. Give yourself permission to write with abandon, free from the constraints of perfectionism or self-doubt. Embrace the messiness of the creative process, knowing that you can always revise and refine your work later. The most important thing is to get your ideas down on paper and let your imagination run wild.

Step 5: Revise and Refine
Once you've completed your first draft, it's time to roll up your sleeves and dive into the revision process. Review your manuscript with a critical eye, focusing on plot holes, character development, pacing, and language. Seek feedback from trusted beta readers or writing groups, and be open to constructive criticism. Remember, writing is rewriting, and each round of revisions brings you closer to realizing your vision.

Step 6: Polish Your Prose
As you approach the final stages of your book, pay close attention to the finer details of your prose. Polish your writing for clarity, coherence, and style, ensuring that every word serves a purpose and resonates with your readers. Fine-tune your dialogue, descriptive passages, and narrative voice to create a compelling and immersive reading experience.

Step 7: Embrace the Publishing Process
With your manuscript polished to perfection, it's time to explore your publishing options. Whether you choose traditional publishing, self-publishing, or a hybrid approach, do your research and weigh the pros and cons of each path. Invest in professional editing, cover design, and formatting to ensure that your book meets industry standards and stands out in a crowded marketplace.

Step 8: Celebrate Your Achievement
Finally, take a moment to celebrate your achievement and acknowledge the hard work and dedication that went into writing your book. Whether you host a launch party, share your success on social media, or simply treat yourself to a well-deserved indulgence, savor the joy of seeing your words in print and the impact they have on readers around the world.

Remember, writing a book is not just about the destination—it's about the journey of self-discovery, growth, and transformation that unfolds along the way. Embrace the challenges, embrace the triumphs, and above all, embrace the power of storytelling to change hearts and minds. Your masterpiece awaits—so pick up your pen, unleash your creativity, and write the book you were born to write.

Author Chantelle Crowell

Finding Your Path: Embracing Growth and Individuality, Inspired by Chantelle Crowell's *Journey*

Life's challenges can often leave us feeling uncertain and lost, but these moments are key opportunities for growth. In Chantelle Crowell's book, [Book Title], she shares how overcoming personal, professional, and societal obstacles taught her resilience and strength. Her journey reminds us that challenges, though daunting, are essential for self-discovery and growth.

A central theme in Chantelle's story is embracing individuality. She encourages readers to stop comparing themselves to others and to celebrate what makes them unique. By staying true to ourselves, we can live more authentic, fulfilling lives.

Chantelle also emphasizes the importance of pursuing dreams with passion and dedication. Her inspiring path shows that while the road may be tough, the rewards of perseverance are profound.

Discover more about Chantelle Crowell's powerful journey and how to find your path by reading her book on Amazon here. Believe in yourself and never stop pursuing your dreams.

Explore We Wake! by Chantelle Crowell: A Powerful Journey of Healing

Chantelle Crowell's We Wake is a captivating exploration of personal healing, self-discovery, and resilience. Through heartfelt storytelling, Crowell navigates the deep emotions of loss, love, and renewal, offering readers a reflective and empowering journey. This book serves as a guide for those seeking to overcome life's challenges and embrace the power of awakening to their true selves. We Wake is not just a book; it's a transformative experience that encourages readers to heal and grow. Discover this profound work on Amazon here and be inspired by its message of hope.

Discover Chantelle Crowell's Alkebu-lan: A Journey of Heritage and Empowerment

Alkebu-lan by Chantelle Crowell is an inspiring and thought-provoking book that explores the rich history and cultural significance of the ancient African civilization, Alkebu-lan. Crowell delves into the forgotten legacy of this powerful region, bringing its stories, wisdom, and heritage to life. Through her vivid storytelling, she not only reclaims Africa's historical narrative but also empowers readers to embrace their roots and heritage with pride. Alkebu-lan is a must-read for those looking to deepen their understanding of African history and its lasting impact on modern society. Find it on Amazon

Shenita Yell is a passionate Inspirational Speaker and Life Coach with over 20 years of experience in the Women's Ministry. She is currently the Executive Director for the nonprofit organization, Galveston County Sisterhood where she successfully inspires and motivates women of all ages to unify in love as they combat the issues of their lives, relationships, and communities.

She is also the CEO of the Gospel Depot Fashion Boutique, where she inspires others to not only feel good but to look good as well. Shenita holds an Associates of Arts degree in Secondary Education and a Bachelor of Business Administration degree. Her expertise is Business Management, of which she has over 30 years of experience.

She has managed over 100 employees at a time within the Retail industry. In her free time, Shenita enjoys spending quality time with her family and spoiling her grandkids.

To get a copy, ordering information below.

THE TARNISHED CROWN

"*Rising From the Wreckage of a Mother's Drug Addiction*"

Just because God woke you up THIS morning, doesn't mean He's going to wake you up IN the morning! So let's give him a "right now" praise!!

I am just a Mouthpiece for The Master

BOOKING INFORMATION:
(409) 904-6228
shenitala@gmail.com
Shenita Yell(FACEBOOK)
shenitayell(INSTAGRAM)

To Order Book:
https://ahiddenfigurescollective.com/shenita-yell

AUTHOR

Davina Ward

Davina Ward is an Author and Certified Christian Life Coach commissioned by God to free women and help them understand that resilience is possible - no matter what they have endured. She has experienced a vast array of challenges that have authenticated and motivated her to share her experiences with other vulnerable women.

She commonly refers to herself as the P.U.S.H. Coach, (Persist, Until, Satan, Halts), due to her effective coaching approach that guides women into learning how to discover and tap into their purpose through the tearing down of their limiting beliefs and insecurities.

Her program and teachings provide strategies to remove layers of lies, doubt, and shame that paralyze women of purpose.

Davina partners with her clients as they shift their focus from the reflection they see in the mirror to the warrior God designed them to be in the spirit. Her main goal is personal development leaving her clients feeling equipped and worthy to walk into what God has purposed them to do and be.

Her true passion lies in walking beside vulnerable women to awaken their inner selves as they enter into their destiny.

In addition to her life's work, Davina has an extensive background in the public sector working with individuals with modest means. She was born and raised in New Jersey and resides with her husband, Reverend Robert Ward. She delights in being a mother to 3 sons and a grandmother to 2 grandchildren. She delights in serving in her local church and community.

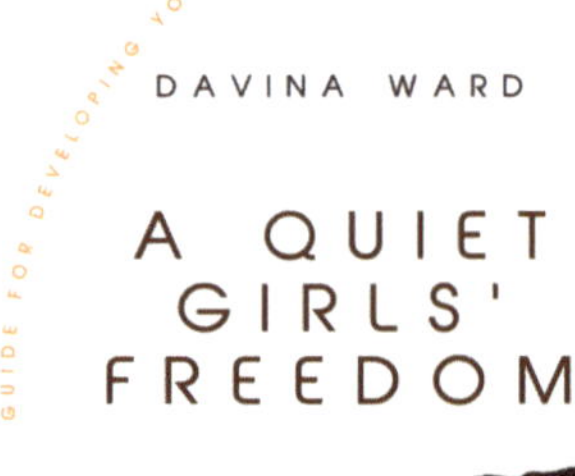

Poetry is Life!

Poetry, often described as the language of the soul, has a unique ability to transcend time, culture, and circumstance, leaving an indelible mark on the hearts and minds of those who encounter its verses. Beyond the rhythmic words and metaphors lies a profound power that has shaped societies, moved nations, and connected individuals on a deeply emotional level. Let's delve into the mystical world of poetry and explore the extraordinary power it holds.

****1. The Healing Elixir**: Poetry possesses a remarkable therapeutic quality. In times of sorrow, it can be a soothing balm, offering solace and a means of expression for emotions too profound for ordinary words. The act of crafting verses can be cathartic, helping individuals process grief, anxiety, or even joy, and find inner peace through self-expression.

****2. The Bridge Between Souls:** Poetry has a unique ability to connect people across cultural, linguistic, and geographical divides. It transcends the boundaries of language, allowing individuals from diverse backgrounds to understand and empathize with one another's experiences. It serves as a universal language that reminds us of our shared humanity.

****3. A Lens to the World:** Poets often act as society's mirrors, reflecting its beauty, flaws, and contradictions. Through verse, they shed light on societal issues, injustices, and human conditions that might otherwise remain unseen. Poetry challenges the status quo and fosters a collective awareness, driving change and sparking movements for justice and equality.

****4. The Dance of Imagination:** Poetry is a playground for imagination. It encourages us to see the world through fresh eyes, to explore the mysteries of existence, and to question the norms of society. It unlocks the doors to creativity, inviting us to wander through the realms of fantasy and the possibilities of the unknown.

****5. A Timeless Legacy:** Poems are timeless treasures. The verses of poets from centuries past continue to resonate with readers today. The enduring quality of poetry lies in its ability to capture the essence of the human experience, making it relevant across generations and eras.

P O E T R Y   I S   L I F E !   (C O N T ' D)

*6. **A Vehicle for Social Change:** Poetry has historically played a pivotal role in driving social change. Poets like Langston Hughes, Maya Angelou, and Pablo Neruda used their verses to advocate for civil rights, equality, and justice. Through their words, they ignited movements and inspired generations to stand up for what they believed in.

7. **The Elevation of Language: Poetry elevates language to an art form. It demonstrates the beauty of precision and the magic of metaphor. Poets carefully select words, creating a symphony of sounds and meanings that delight the senses and challenge the mind.

8. **An Echo of Identity: Poetry is a profound expression of identity. It allows individuals to embrace and celebrate their cultural heritage, personal experiences, and individual uniqueness. It serves as a repository of cultural memory, preserving traditions and stories for future generations.

In a world often dominated by prose and pragmatism, poetry stands as a testament to the enduring power of human creativity and expression. It serves as a bridge between hearts, a beacon of hope, and a catalyst for change. Through its profound ability to heal, connect, and inspire, poetry remains a force that continues to shape the world, one verse at a time.

Dr. Lisa L. Campbell

Dr. Lisa L. Campbell

Dr. Lisa L. Campbell, known as "The Growth Motivator™," is the author of the inspirational book "Grow With Me." In this book, Dr. Lisa shares her journey of overcoming significant personal and professional challenges. Through vivid storytelling and heartfelt reflections, she shares her life lessons on resilience, faith, and personal growth. Her journey as an author began with a desire to inspire others, and she has developed a motivational writing style that connects deeply with readers. "Grow With Me" encourages readers to shed the weight of their burdens, embrace change, and pursue their dreams with determination and confidence. Dr. Lisa's engaging narrative and genuine voice make her book an uplifting and transformative read.

DR. LISA L. CAMPBELL

An interview with Dr. Lisa L. Campbell

I had the pleasure of interviewing Dr. Lisa L. Campbell on **The Author's Lounge Podcast YouTube,** we explored her remarkable journey as a healthcare administrator who has transitioned into the world of writing and podcasting.

Dr. Campbell hosts the inspiring podcast series **"52 Authors in 52 Weeks,"on Youtube** where she features a diverse range of authors, sharing their experiences and insights. During our conversation, she reflected on her passion for writing, highlighting how she continues to push forward with her creative journey. Dr. Campbell's dedication to both her career and storytelling demonstrates her commitment to lifelong learning and growth.

Healthy Living *and* Stress Management

by Valerie Staton

Managing stress in this ever-changing world of ours is for many an immense challenge. Inflation, job insecurity, healthcare issues, violence, homelessness, financial woes, workload, personal relationship problems, health issues, disease and death are some of the stressors faced by today's society.

Stress is often a precursor to physical and mental health issues. Chronic stress can lead to a myriad of symptoms such as headache, heartburn, fatigue, sleep deprivation, irritability, high blood pressure, lack of appetite, pain, body ache, stroke and/or heart attack.

The adage "You are what you eat" has a degree of truth to it. Maintaining a healthy diet consisting of fruit, vegetables, whole grains and lean protein is important for overall health. A reduction in caffeine and alcohol consumption is beneficial to one's health as well.

Incorporating whole grains such as barley, rye, rice, quinoa, corn, oats, whole wheat, bulgar and sorghum, provides the body nutrients, fiber, minerals and vitamins. Whole grains lower cholesterol, blood pressure, insulin levels, and help control weight loss.

Lean proteins such as Greek yogurt, lean beef, chicken, turkey and fish, tofu, lentils, beans, peas, edamame, and eggs, lowers blood pressure and cholesterol levels. They also reduce the risk of heart disease and support the body's immune system.

Walking for at least thirty minutes a day is a good way to reduce stress. Rest, relaxation, physical exercise, yoga, Tai Chi, meditation, visualization, biofeedback, soothing music, massage therapy, and deep breathing exercises, are some healthy ways to decrease stress. Deep breathing exercises are known to lower the heart rate and relieve muscle tension.

Healthy Living *and* *Stress Management* Cont'd

by Valerie Staton

Another way to manage stress is by saying "NO" to requests that create stress. Set limits to maintain a peaceful state of mind. Remove yourself from the cause of stress to an environment that evokes feelings of peace and tranquility, i.e., a park, a comfortable bench by a burbling river or rolling stream. Engage in activities that bring you joy. Read a good book, watch a movie alone or with a friend. Surround yourself with positive thinking people.

If you've tried all the above and are still stressed out, it may be time to talk to a professional. Seek help immediately via your primary physician or any of the free helplines, that provide free, confidential help to those needing their support. Most free helplines are staffed by counselors or volunteers and are accessible 24 hours a day, 7 days a week. Services are offered over the phone, via chat and/or text message.

WHAT'S COOKING?

COLLARD GREENS WITH SMOKED TURKEY

Ingredients:

- 1 bunch collard greens, stems removed and chopped

- 1 pound smoked turkey, chopped

- 1 onion, chopped

- 2 cloves garlic, minced

- 1 tablespoon apple cider vinegar

- 1 teaspoon smoked paprika

- 1/2 teaspoon black pepper

- 1/4 cup water

- Salt to taste

Instructions:

1. In a large pot, bring water to a boil. Add collard greens and cook for 5-7 minutes, or until tender. Drain and set aside.

2. In the same pot, sauté onion and garlic until softened.

3. Add smoked turkey, apple cider vinegar, smoked paprika, black pepper, and water. Bring to a simmer and cook for 10-15 minutes, or until flavors have combined.

4. Add cooked collard greens to the pot and toss to coat. Season with salt to taste.

FRIED CHICKEN WITH BUTTERMILK CORNBREAD

Ingredients:

- 1 whole chicken, cut into pieces
- 1 cup buttermilk
- 1 cup all-purpose flour
- 1/2 cup cornmeal
- 1 teaspoon salt
- 1/2 teaspoon black pepper
- 1/4 teaspoon garlic powder
- 1/4 teaspoon onion powder
- Vegetable oil for frying

For Buttermilk Cornbread:

- 1 cup cornmeal
- 1 cup all-purpose flour
- 1 tablespoon sugar
- 2 teaspoons baking powder
- 1/2 teaspoon salt
- 1 cup buttermilk
- 1 egg
- 2 tablespoons melted butter

Instructions:

1. Fried Chicken: In a large bowl, marinate chicken pieces in buttermilk for at least 30 minutes.
2. In a separate bowl, combine flour, cornmeal, salt, pepper, garlic powder, and onion powder.
3. Dredge chicken pieces in flour mixture.
4. Heat vegetable oil in a large skillet over medium-high heat.
5. Fry chicken pieces until golden brown and cooked through.
6. Buttermilk Cornbread: Preheat oven to 350°F (175°C).
7. In a large bowl, whisk together cornmeal, flour, sugar, baking powder, and salt.
8. Stir in buttermilk, egg, and melted butter.
9. Pour batter into a greased 9x9 inch baking pan.
10. Bake for 20-25 minutes, or until a toothpick inserted into the center comes out clean.

SWEET POTATO PIE

Sweet Potato Pie

Ingredients:

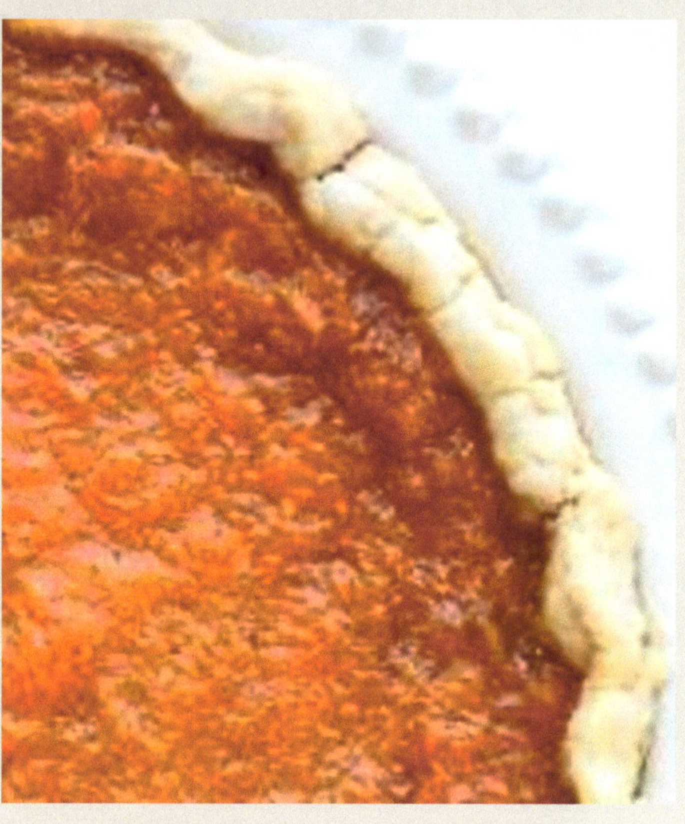

- 1 (9-inch) pie crust
- 2 large sweet potatoes, peeled and cubed
- 1 cup granulated sugar
- 1/2 cup packed brown sugar
- 1/4 cup butter, melted
- 2 large eggs
- 1/4 cup milk
- 1 teaspoon vanilla extract
- 1/2 teaspoon ground cinnamon
- 1/4 teaspoon ground nutmeg
- 1/4 teaspoon ground ginger
- 1/8 teaspoon salt

Instructions:

1. Preheat oven to 350°F (175°C).
2. Roll out pie crust and place in a 9-inch pie plate.
3. Bake crust for 10 minutes or until lightly golden.
4. In a large bowl, combine sweet potatoes, granulated sugar, brown sugar, melted butter, eggs, milk, vanilla extract, cinnamon, nutmeg, ginger, and salt. Beat until smooth.
5. Pour filling into the pre-baked pie crust.
6. Bake for 45-50 minutes, or until a knife inserted into the center comes out clean.
7. Let cool completely before serving.

Literary
MOMENTS & RESOURCES

A One-Stop Shop
For Authors

AUTHORPRENEURSHIP 101 COURSE FOR AUTHORS!

- **A GUIDED COURSE TO HELP YOU COMPLETE & PUBLISH YOUR BOOK**
- **CLASSES BEGIN – JAN 2025**

REGISTER:EDUCATION@BLACKWOMENAUTHORS.NET

Lead by Paulette Henson and Michelle Hardy (@SolitudeWithMichelle)

At BWA, our goal is to educate new and blossoming writers on how to write and publish books.

Whether you are just budding, wanting to finally complete a writing project, or already seasoned, we're more than happy to help you on your journey from writing to publishing your book.

BWA proudly announces its first course to help our strong community build the best possible quality book for its members and their target audience. Author Preneurship 101 taught by Professor Paulette Henson and Michelle Hardy is an author business writing course designed to help new and seasoned authors get published in a one-stop shop. Being a new author can be challenging, but BWA is here to make things go as smoothly as possible with a complete writing and publishing process. For information or to register send an email to:

Education@blackwomenauthors.net

TIP OF THE MONTH

Many of us as authors, want to price our book based on looks. We'll say "I think my book should be $XYZ.99," because it looks good; however we need to remember your book is only going to sell based on how well you market it, the quality information you provide, and its appropriate price in the marketplace. The price point for your type of book is not based on how you are feeling that day. Take time to research the books in your genre and see what the price points are for print, digital (ebook) and audio so you can be competitive.

66 *Knowing your Power is Power* **99**
Michelle Hardy

Embrace YOUR VOICE!

A Column for Aspiring Black Women Authors

BY VICTORIA PEARSON

Hello, fellow writers and dreamers!

My name is Victoria Pearson and I am excited to announce this new monthly column for Black Women Authors Magazine and navigate with you the unique world of Black women authors in this new monthly column.

Whether you are a seasoned writer or just starting out, this space is for us—a place to celebrate our stories, discuss our challenges, and lift each other up.

What to Expect

In each issue, I'll share insights about best practices, how-to guidance, and other information that may be helpful to you on this journey. I'm also eager to hear your insights. We'll delve into the importance of self-care for writers, offer practical tips for honing your craft, and explore the rapidly-changing world of self-publishing. We'll also discuss the unique challenges and opportunities Black women face in the literary world, and I'll provide resources and advice to help you succeed.

Why This Column Matters?

In a literary landscape that doesn't always reflect our rich experiences, it's time for Black women to unapologetically own our narratives. I created this column to provide a haven, a place to learn, grow, discuss strategies for increasing representation, overcoming bias, and building our digital platforms. We'll tackle everything from mental well-being and writer's block to the nitty-gritty of the publishing world. I welcome ideas about future topics of interest to you.

Your Voice Matters

This column is a conversation. I want to hear your thoughts, questions, and experiences. Feel free to reach out to me on the new BWA Facebook subgroup with your feedback. I am also new on this journey, so I'm here to listen, learn, and grow alongside you.

Health Notes

For Thanksgiving Dinner

As the air turns crisp and the holiday season approaches, it's the perfect time to turn our attention inward and focus on our overall health and wellbeing. This month, and every month moving forward, our new Health Notes section will dive deep into the latest trends, tips, and techniques to help you achieve optimal mental, physical, and spiritual health.

Let's start with arguably the most celebrated holiday of the year - Thanksgiving. While the turkey, stuffing, and pumpkin pie may be the stars of the show, it's important to remember that true nourishment goes far beyond what's on your plate. This Thanksgiving, we challenge you to approach the holiday with intention and gratitude.

First, be mindful of the ingredients you're using to prepare your Thanksgiving feast. Opt for organic, locally-sourced produce and pasture-raised meats to ensure you're fueling your body with the most nutrient-dense foods. Not only will this make your meal healthier, but it also supports your local community.

As you gather around the table, be present and engaged in the conversations happening. Ask thoughtful questions, listen intently, and make meaningful connections with your loved ones. This quality time together is just as vital to your wellbeing as the meal itself. Take a moment to go around the table and share what you're most grateful for - this ritual of expressing gratitude has been shown to increase feelings of joy and contentment.

Finally, don't forget to nourish your soul. Whether it's through prayer, meditation, or simply spending time in nature, find ways to cultivate a sense of inner peace and calm. This quiet reflection will help you approach the new year with clarity, focus, and a renewed sense of purpose.

By honoring all aspects of your health this Thanksgiving, you'll not only enjoy a more fulfilling holiday experience, but you'll also set the stage for a healthier, happier you in the months to come. We're so excited to embark on this journey together. Here's to your best health yet!

Good health!   P.K. Wilson

The Author's Lounge

W/PAULETTE

Next Guest Author: You!

PROMOTE YOUR BOOK !

FOR MORE DETAILS

EMAIL:THEAUTHORSLOUNGETVSHOW@GMAIL.COM

WATCH ON FACEBOOK
(LIVE) BLACK WOMEN
AUTHORS
& YOUTUBE

LIKE/COMMENT/SHARE/SUBSCRIBE

Granny's Corner

Hey Y'all,

My granddaughter who is still in diapers really likes books. She makes baby sounds and inaudible baby words out loud as that is her way of reading (she is mimicking her older sisters who often read aloud).

When she is 'reading' she is content to sit on the floor and flip through each page. Quietly, I rotate her books, exchanging them so when she grabs one, often it is a different story. At some point she will come across a book that she is already familiar with, as I have placed it back into the rotation (I'm just keeping her interested). Also, while she is 'reading' it gives me a bit of time to do other things in the kitchen or whatever.

This particular day, she was 'reading' a familiar book that I had placed back into the rotation. At one point she became agitated and crawled into the kitchen where I was. The entire time she was trying to tell me something, but she doesn't really have a vocabulary, yet. I was not able to figure out what she was saying so I told her to show me. So, she crawled, and I followed, back to her book.

She was fussy and making sounds as she handed me the book. Instantly I realized a couple of pages were stuck together. At the same time she was showing me this problem and making her inaudible words, the pitch in her voice was rising. I gathered that she was fussing, at me, as if I had messed up her book.

I just stared at this little person without saying a word. My private thoughts were that it was likely a result from her own little sticky fingers. Nonetheless, after a moment of our staredown, I separated the pages and gave her back her book.

She looked up at me, now settled, and in clear Baby speak she said, "tank yu Gra-ee".
I replied, "you're welcome", then I turned and walked back into the kitchen. Whew - crisis over!
  By A. Williams

"All my grandbabies love books"

Photography by Craig A. Kirkland
Great Amazement Multimedia Entertainment LLC

Native New Yorker Living in Rhode Island Celebrates the Success of Her First Book

CLARISE ANNETTE BROOKS knew from a young age that she could spark magic when she put pen to paper. "I recall when our teachers would give us creative writing assignments in elementary school. We each had to take turns reading our work at the front of the room. My classmates often requested that I go first," Clarise recalls. "I knew I had them when they laughed at the right moment, gasped at the right time, and talked with me later about the characters I had created or about the poetry that I had just performed for them. It came easy to me and I enjoyed it SO MUCH. It has always been fun to use imagery to create a scene, alliteration to develop a flow of words, or repetition to demand emphasis. These tools of the language helped me to take my classmates on a journey with me and planted the seed for my lifelong love of performing my work before a live audience. I learned how to use language and its tools to touch the minds and spirits of others."

Erica N. Bryant is a wife and mother of two. She is an elementary educator and literacy advocate. Erica is the president and founder of Sparrow's Song Ministries (Sparrowssongministries.com), a group of believers who "just love Jesus." Her campaign: "The Word W.O.R.K.S." have helped women renew and strengthen their relationship with God by falling in love with His Word. Erica serves faithfully at her home church, Strait Gate Deliverance Center, where her father, Bishop Jerome Rogers, is pastor.

The Art of the Hook: How to Start Your Story Strong: The Power of First Impressions

By Victoria H. Pearson

In a world overflowing with content, the first few lines of your writing are more critical than ever. Whether it's a novel, a short story, an article, or a social media post, how you begin can determine if your audience stays engaged or moves on. The hook—the opening line or lines of your work—is essential in capturing attention and piquing interest. But what exactly is a hook, and how can you master the art of writing one that resonates with your audience?

What is a Hook?

A "hook" is the compelling first line of any piece of writing that grabs the reader's attention. This concept transcends written words; it applies to speeches, films, and even songs. A great hook can set the tone for what follows, drawing readers into your narrative and making them want to know more. Much like a fisherman's bait, a well-crafted hook lures your audience in and keeps them engaged.

Why a Strong Hook Matters

A strong hook is more than just a clever opening line; it's the foundation upon which your entire piece is built. Research shows that readers often decide within the first few sentences whether they will continue reading . A powerful hook can:

- Capture Attention: Instantly draw in your audience and spark their curiosity.
- Set the Tone: Establish the mood and style of your writing, whether it be serious, humorous, or thought-provoking.
- Create a Connection: Engage readers on an emotional level, making them more invested in your narrative.

The Anatomy of a Hook

Hooks can take many forms, and different types can be effective for different writing styles and genres. Here are some categories of hooks, each with its own unique appeal:

1. The Surprising Statistic Hook
Presenting an unexpected fact can create intrigue and encourage readers to explore the topic further. For example:
"Did you know that over 700,000 children enter foster care in the U.S. every year? That's enough children to fill a small city."
Example: An article on child welfare used a surprising statistic about the number of children in foster care, prompting readers to consider the systemic issues at play.

2. The Provocative Question Hook
Asking a thought-provoking question challenges readers and invites them to think critically about the topic. For instance:
"What if the next great innovation in technology comes from someone you've never heard of?"
Example: A technology magazine began an article about underrepresented voices in tech with this question, sparking discussions around diversity and inclusion in the industry.

3. The Famous Quote Hook
Using a powerful quote from a well-known figure can lend authority and resonance to your writing. For example:
"As Maya Angelou once said, 'There is no greater agony than bearing an untold story inside you.'"
Example: A personal essay about the challenges of storytelling opened with this quote, immediately establishing a connection with readers who may have their own untold stories.

4. The Bold Statement Hook
Starting with a strong assertion can engage readers right away. For instance:
"Every writer struggles with self-doubt, but only the brave conquer it."
Example: A blog post on overcoming writer's block opened with this statement, setting a motivational tone for aspiring writers.

5. The Importance Hook
Explaining why your topic matters at the outset can compel readers to stay engaged. For instance:
"In a world where attention spans are shrinking, mastering the art of the hook is crucial for every writer."
Example: A writing workshop advertisement highlighted the significance of hooks, prompting attendees to enroll for practical tips.

6. The Anecdotal Hook
Sharing a personal story or anecdote can create a relatable entry point. For example:
"When I was a child, my grandmother used to tell me stories that transported me to other worlds."
Example: An article on storytelling techniques began with a personal childhood memory, inviting readers to reflect on their own experiences with storytelling.

Example: A mystery novel's blurb utilized a cliffhanger to intrigue potential readers and encourage them to dive into the story.

The Role of the Hook in Different Genres

Understanding how hooks function in various genres can help you tailor your approach. Here's a breakdown of how to apply hooks in specific contexts:

Fiction

In fiction, hooks are vital for immersing readers in the story. Whether it's the opening line of a novel or a short story, you want to create a sense of intrigue that makes readers invested in the characters and plot.

Example: A fantasy novel may open with a vivid description of an otherworldly landscape, setting the stage for adventure.

Non-Fiction

For non-fiction, hooks can draw readers into factual narratives or persuasive essays. By presenting statistics or asking questions, writers can engage their audience's curiosity.

Example: A health article may begin with an alarming statistic about a rising health issue, compelling readers to learn more about prevention.

Personal Essays

In personal essays, hooks often center around relatable anecdotes or quotes that resonate emotionally with readers. These hooks help establish a personal connection.

Example: A personal essay on resilience may start with a quote about overcoming adversity, setting a reflective tone.

Techniques for Crafting Effective Hooks

Creating a compelling hook requires practice and experimentation. Here are some techniques to consider:

Know Your Audience: Tailor your hook to resonate with the interests and preferences of your target readers.

Be Authentic: Your unique voice and perspective are your greatest assets. Let them shine through in your hook.

Experiment with Structure: Try different types of hooks in your writing to see which ones elicit the best responses from your audience.

Revise and Refine: Don't be afraid to revise your hooks. Sometimes, the strongest hooks emerge during the editing process.

Read Widely: Expose yourself to various genres and styles to understand what works and what doesn't in terms of hooks.

Case Studies: Hooks That Worked

Examining successful examples can provide inspiration for your writing. Here are some notable hooks that have captivated audiences:

"The Catcher in the Rye" by J.D. Salinger: The iconic opening line, "If you really want to hear about it, the first thing you'll probably want to know is where I was born, and what my lousy childhood was like," invites readers into Holden Caulfield's world, making them curious about his story.

"A Tale of Two Cities" by Charles Dickens: Dickens starts with, "It was the best of times, it was the worst of times," immediately creating a sense of intrigue and setting the stage for the novel's themes.

BuzzFeed Articles: Many BuzzFeed articles begin with relatable anecdotes or humorous observations, such as, "If you've ever tried to make dinner after a long day at work, you know the struggle is real." This creates an instant connection with readers.

Conclusion: Mastering the Art of the Hook

Crafting an effective hook is an invaluable skill for any writer. The opening lines of your work set the stage for everything that follows, and a well-executed hook can

make all the difference in capturing and retaining your audience's attention. By experimenting with different types of hooks and understanding their application across genres, you can enhance your writing and engage readers from the very first line.

As you embark on your writing journey, remember the power of the hook. With practice, you can develop the skill to create compelling openings that resonate deeply with your audience, drawing them into the rich worlds you create with your words.

Sources

[1] K.A. Elam, "How Long Do Readers Stay Engaged? A Study of Reader Retention on News Websites," Journal of Digital Media, 2022.

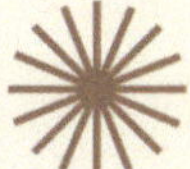

Author
Latasha Hales

Bio:

Latasha About the author: Latasha is a minister, an educator, a professionalism and life coach, a business owner, an inspirational speaker but most of all, a child of the Most High God. Her desire is to help as many people as possible on this journey we call life.

These journals were created with people like me in mind. You know what you need but you are not always sure where to find it. Those of us on a journey to go deeper in our walk with God but just need a little help. It is my sincere desire that this journal helps you on your path and becomes another tool in your toolbox of life. I pray these scriptures, reflections, confirmations and affirmations become a part of you every day life. Be bless!

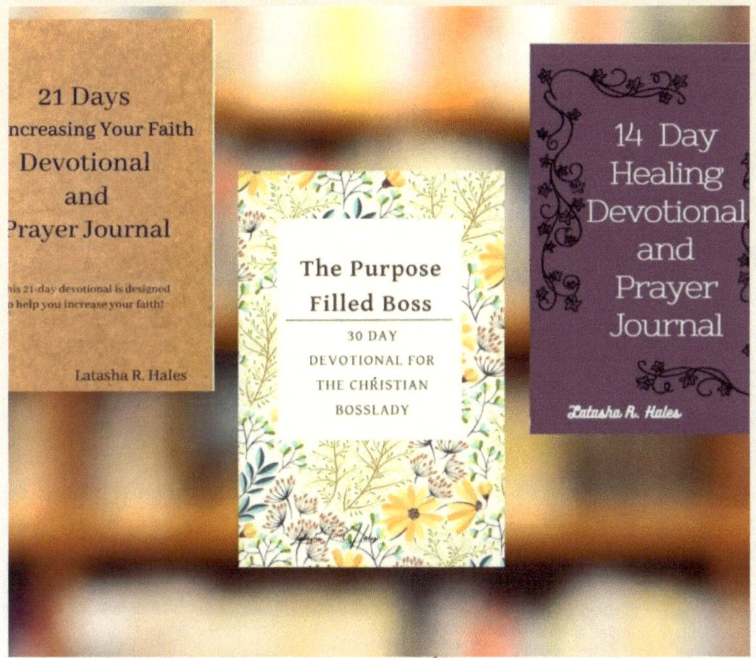

Royal Ross is a native of Jersey City, New Jersey, the oldest of 16 siblings, mother, and grandmother. Royal is the first in her family to obtain a college degree.

She holds the following degrees: Associate in Accounting, Bachelor in Accounting, Master in Accounting, and an MBA in Management. Royal is an Entrepreneur, Author, Evangelist, and Speaker. Her Senior Pastor, Bishop Jevah Richardson and Lady Marcy Richardson where she serves as Elder, of A Better Life Ministry.

The Founder of Mother's Unite in Prayer conference dial-in prayer call. The CEO of She Is Pretty Strong LLC, The Founder of Heart For People Ministry Inc. She's a Yoga/Fitness Coach, In addition, she is a Full Time Admissions Recruiter and Part Time Business and Accounting Instructor. She's currently completing her dissertation, Doctor In Educational Leadership.

Elder Royal Ross' motto is followed through one of her favorite scriptures: "I can do all things through Christ which strengtheneth me." Philippians 4:13

Contact

Email: rossdroyal@gmail.com or rross@hccc.edu

Facebook: Royal Ross

Instagram: _sheisprettystrong
_sheisprettystrongllc
_heartforpeopleministryinc

Dial In: Mother's Unite In Prayer each Monday at 7AM Est. 909.318.7652

Heart For People Ministry Prayer Group each Monday at 7:30AM-8:15AM Est. Zoom Info: Meeting ID: 89412437009 Passcode: 514663

Book purchase:
Amazon.com
Barnesandnoble.com
xlibris.com

This 40-page story is a metaphorical gem.

It is a journey for your senses, and it is worth taking!

This is my gift to anyone who has ever experienced losing a loved one.

The South Side Of Heaven

By Stella Stella

Stella Stella

Many required readings in college included commonly known American Literaries (i.e. Hemingway, Poe, Steinbeck, Wells, etc.). All were great writers and I have no knocks against them. However, their stories were too abstract for my life. Within the realm of Literature, there is room for those/us who have a different background, a different perspective, and a passion for reading and writing".

A
WIDOW
AND A
FRIEND
STELLA STELLA

MICHELE HOSKINS

Meet Michele Hoskins, a seasoned educator, leadership development trainer, and dynamic motivational speaker with over three decades of experience. Alongside her husband Paul, Michele is a thriving Urban Air Adventure Park Franchisee, managing two bustling parks in San Antonio while gearing up for an exciting new business venture in 2024.

Michele's journey is a testament to her relentless innovation and purpose-driven action. Her diverse background, which includes being a licensed Minister, former McDonald's Franchisee, accomplished Author, College Professor, and dedicated community leader, reflects her wide-ranging expertise. She recently launched Maintain Momentum, a company poised to make waves, and is on the verge of releasing her upcoming books, "Unshrunk Bacon" and "Love That Works, Works!"

Michele's expertise extends to designing and implementing successful business models, fueled by her strategic vision and keen understanding of organizational dynamics. Her proficiency in setting and achieving goals, coupled with her knack for forging meaningful connections, positions her as a beacon of excellence in business and leadership.

BWA
AUTHOR

AKIYA MASTON

Biography:

Akiya Maston earned her B.A. in Psychology, and an M.A. in Human Resources. After working in Corporate America for several years, she switched careers and found her calling as an educator. She taught high school for 10 years, then obtained her Educational Specialist degree and worked as an administrator for middle and elementary schools for 9 years. She is currently the principal at Pinewoods Elementary School in Estero, Florida.

During her 19 years working in education, she developed several educational resources, one is Music to Mastery, which helps elementary students learn Geography through 11 short songs and maps (www.MusicToMastery.com), and the other is, The Wonder Years of Middle School (www.WonderYearsBook.com).

Akiya Maston's Middle School Story:

During Akiya Maston's middle school years, she was never bullied but was a bystander to twin girls who were bullied nearly every day. She chose not to get involved for fear of being the new target. So, what did she do? Rationalized the bullying. "Well, if they dressed differently, acted differently, styled their hair differently then they wouldn't be getting picked on." This was 35 years ago and her own behavior, her lack of getting involved to help, still haunts Akiya to this day. Years ago, the age old mantra was "stick and stones may break my bones, but words will never harm me," We know now that words can be more hurtful, and the pain can also last longer with words. In the chapter, Bullying and Bystander Effect, Akiya shares the full story along with tips to help students and parents navigate scenarios such as these. Unlike, 1988, students not only face this type of torment but now there is also a social media component. So taunting lasts beyond the school walls.

Victoria Anderson is an emerging voice in the field of self-discovery and empowerment, celebrated for her unique perspective on healing from childhood trauma and defying societal expectations. Her story is deeply intertwined with her own experiences of overcoming obstacles that sought to limit her potential. Growing up in a vibrant yet challenging urban setting, Victoria encountered societal stereotypes that attempted to confine her dreams. However, her unwavering determination to break free from these constraints led her to pursue education as a means of transcending boundaries.

After graduating from a prominent university, Victoria embarked on a personal quest to understand the complexities of childhood trauma and societal pressures. Motivated by her struggles and the stories of individuals she encountered, she devoted herself to extensive research and introspection, seeking ways to facilitate healing and personal growth.

Victoria's writing reflects her deep understanding of the human experience, infused with empathy and wisdom. Through her work, she aims to guide others toward self-discovery and overcoming adversity, offering insights and strategies for navigating life's challenges.

As a passionate advocate for mental health and personal development, Victoria extends her impact beyond her writing. She engages in speaking engagements, captivating audiences with her authentic storytelling and empowering messages. Additionally, she actively participates in community outreach programs, mentoring and supporting young people as they navigate their paths toward resilience and empowerment.

Victoria Anderson's commitment to fostering healing, reshaping perspectives, and nurturing resilience serves as an inspiration to those grappling with childhood trauma and societal pressures. Her dedication to igniting transformation and instilling hope continues to influence and uplift individuals on their journeys of self-discovery.

AUTHOR VALERIE STATON

Valerie D. Staton is an author/poet from New Jersey. She has written three insightful books and has contributed poetry and short stories to several books, anthologies, and online communities.

Her latest publication entitled "Journey to Wellness: A Personal Health Recordkeeper " is an excellent resource for keeping track of health related information.

Her second publication, "Staton the Facts - The Informative Bible-Based Activity Book" has over 1,200 activities. Readers will find within its pages word scrambles, word matches, word searches, speaker identification, bible verse completion and scripture based cryptogram puzzles to solve. Also included throughout this spectacular book are over one hundred fun biblical facts. Answer sheets in the back of the book contain reference text.

The author's first publication, "Odes of Praise - A Collection of Christian Poetry, consists of 86 awe-inspiring poems, edifying our Lord and Savior Jesus Christ.

These wonderful publications are available for purchase on Amazon.com.

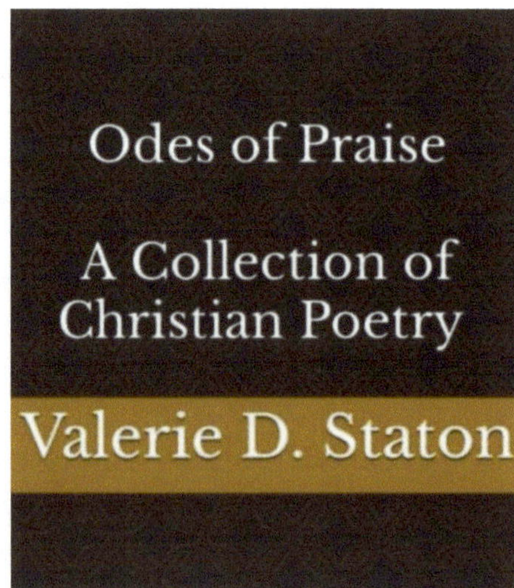

OMEAKIO TUCKER

Bio

Omeakio Tucker, a new and upcoming author, fearlessly shares her personal journey of facing challenges, feeling stuck, and ultimately breaking free in her transformative book. Drawing from her own experiences and her deep connection with God, Omeakio is your cheerleader and guide, showing you that transformation is possible. This book is more than just another self-help guide; it's a heart-to-heart conversation and a loving reminder that you are capable of so much more than you ever thought possible. Omeakio will help you identify the limiting beliefs and patterns that have been holding you back and provide you with the tools you need to unleash your Unstoppable PowHer.

With a Bachelor's Degree in Business Administration, a Master's Degree in Organizational Leadership, and certification as an Executive Coach and Consultant, Omeakio brings a wealth of knowledge and expertise to her writing. Her 20+ years of experience as a dynamic manager, creative director, passionate mentor, and influential executive in Corporate America have shaped her into a captivating mixture of talents, making her an unstoppable force and the ultimate catalyst for meaningful change.

Guided by her unwavering faith and relationship with God, Omeakio pours life and inspiration into the community she serves with steadfast dedication. She resides in Dallas, TX, with her loving husband, six beautiful children, nine precious grandchildren, and the world's cutest grandpup. Her family is her rock and inspiration, providing her with the unwavering support and love that fuels her mission to empower women worldwide.

The Writer's Guide to Staying Healthy: Incorporating Exercise and Healthy Eating

By Paulette Henson

Writing is an intellectually stimulating and creatively fulfilling activity, but it often involves long hours of sitting. While focusing on characters, plot lines, and dialogue, it's easy for writers to neglect their physical health. This guide is designed to help writers incorporate exercise and healthy eating into their routines to maintain both their creative energy and overall well-being.

The Sedentary Challenge of Writing

The nature of writing requires extended periods of sitting and minimal physical activity. This sedentary lifestyle can lead to numerous health issues, including poor posture, back pain, weight gain, and decreased cardiovascular health. However, by integrating simple exercises and mindful eating habits into your daily routine, you can counteract these negative effects and boost your productivity and creativity.

57

Daily Exercise Tips for Writers
1. Desk Exercises:
   - Seated Leg Lifts: While sitting, straighten one leg and hold it parallel to the floor for a few seconds, then lower it. Repeat 10 times for each leg.
   - Chair Squats: Stand up from your chair and then sit back down without using your hands. Repeat 10-15 times.
   - Shoulder Shrugs: Lift your shoulders towards your ears and hold for a few seconds, then release. Repeat 10 times.
2. Stretching Routines:
   - Neck Stretches: Gently tilt your head towards each shoulder and hold for 10-15 seconds to relieve tension.
   - Upper Body Stretch: Raise your arms above your head and interlock your fingers, then stretch upwards. Hold for 15-20 seconds.
   - Back Stretch: Stand up and place your hands on your lower back, then gently arch backwards and hold for 10 seconds.
3. Walking Breaks:
   - Scheduled Walks: Set an alarm to remind you to take a 5-10 minute walk every hour. Use this time to clear your mind and refresh your body.
   - Walking Meetings: If discussing ideas with a writing partner or editor, consider taking a walk while you talk.
4. Home Workouts:
   - Yoga: Practicing yoga can improve flexibility, reduce stress, and enhance focus. Follow online classes or use apps for guided sessions.
   - Bodyweight Exercises: Incorporate push-ups, sit-ups, and planks into your daily routine. These exercises require no equipment and can be done in short bursts throughout the day.

Healthy Eating Tips for Writers
1. Balanced Meals:
   - Include All Food Groups: Ensure your meals contain a balance of lean proteins, whole grains, fruits, vegetables, and healthy fats.
   - Portion Control: Avoid overeating by using smaller plates and being mindful of portion sizes.
2. Healthy Snacks:
   - Fruits and Vegetables: Keep cut-up veggies and fresh fruits on hand for easy, nutritious snacking.
   - Nuts and Seeds: A handful of nuts or seeds provides a healthy dose of protein and fats, helping to keep you full and focused.
3. Hydration:
   - Drink Water Regularly: Keep a water bottle at your desk and take regular sips throughout the day to stay hydrated.
   - Limit Caffeine: While a cup of coffee or tea can boost alertness, excessive caffeine can lead to dehydration and jitteriness.
4. Meal Planning:
   - Prep Ahead: Spend some time each week preparing meals and snacks to avoid reaching for unhealthy options during busy writing sessions.
   - Balanced Diet: Focus on nutrient-rich foods that provide sustained energy and support brain health, such as leafy greens, berries, and fish rich in omega-3 fatty acids.
5. Mindful Eating:
   - Avoid Eating at Your Desk: Take a break to enjoy your meals away from your workspace. This helps you relax and appreciate your food.
   - Listen to Your Body: Pay attention to hunger and fullness cues to prevent overeating or undereating.

<u>Creating a Sustainable Routine</u>

1. Set Realistic Goals:
   - Start Small: Begin with small changes, such as incorporating one exercise and one healthy eating habit into your daily routine.
   - Gradual Progress: Increase the intensity and duration of your exercises gradually to avoid burnout and injury.
2. Combine Writing with Physical Activity:
   - Active Writing: Use a standing desk or balance on an exercise ball while writing to engage your muscles.
   - Creative Movement: Take a break to dance, do jumping jacks, or simply move around your space to boost energy and creativity.
3. Stay Motivated:
   - Track Your Progress: Keep a journal to record your exercise routines and eating habits. Celebrate your achievements, no matter how small.
   - Find a Buddy: Partner with another writer or friend to stay accountable and motivated. Share your goals and progress with each other.
4. Prioritize Self-Care:
   - Rest and Recovery: Ensure you get enough sleep and rest to allow your body to recover and function optimally.
   - Mental Health: Practice mindfulness, meditation, or deep-breathing exercises to reduce stress and maintain mental clarity.
5. Balance and Flexibility:
   - Adapt to Your Schedule: Recognize that some days will be busier than others. Adjust your exercise and eating routines as needed, but strive for consistency.
   - Listen to Your Body: Pay attention to how your body feels and adjust your activities accordingly. Avoid pushing yourself too hard.

By incorporating these exercise and healthy eating tips into your daily routine, you can enhance your physical and mental well-being, ultimately supporting your writing career. Remember, a healthy writer is a productive and creative writer. Embrace these habits and watch as your energy, focus, and overall health improve. Happy writing and stay healthy!

THANKS TO GOD FOR THIS VISION!

With heartfelt gratitude, I lift my voice in thanks to God for his divine vision that has brought such extraordinary authors and poets to my midst. Their brilliance and creativity have enriched my life and the lives of countless others. I am humbled by the gift of their presence and the beauty they bring to the literary world.

I give thanks to God for orchestrating the perfect alignment of circumstances that allowed me to connect with these wonderful souls.

It is a true testament to His divine plan and the power of his guiding hand. I am in awe of the ways in which God has brought us together, weaving a tapestry of talent, wisdom, and inspiration that continues to inspire us all.

In this moment of gratitude, I acknowledge God's grace and providence for granting me the opportunity to collaborate and learn from these gifted authors and poets.

May we continue to be guided by God's wisdom and love as we journey together, united by our shared passion for literature, the written and spoken word.

Paulette R. Henson

In This Edition...

Dr. Lisa L. Campbell Akiya Maston April Mack Wilson April Williams Chantelle Crowell Cheryl Garrison Clarise Annette Brooks Davina Ward Doris Pinkett Elizabeth Michaud Erica N. Bryant Dr. Gracie Kearse-McCastler	Author, FEATURE Author Author Contributor Author Author Author Author Author Author Author Author	Grow With Me Bullying And The Bystander Effect A Journey From Discouragement To Encouragement Granny's Corner Journey, We Wake Up Legacy Excuse Me While I Live My Life A Quiet Girls Freedom Pinke Loved Five Dreams Dwell Remebering With The Forgotten Fruit The Purpose Filled Boss, 14 Day Healing Devotional And Prayer Journal
Latasha Hales	Author	Unshrunk Bacon
Michelle Hoskins	Author	Being Intentional Journal - Purpose Driven
Nia Hunt	Author	Your Unstoppable PowHer - It's Time To Release Her
Omeakio Tucker	Author	Health Notes
P.K. Wilson	Contributor	
Royal Ross	Author	Stay Connected To The True Vine, She Is Pretty Strong
Shenita L. Yell	Co-Author	The Tarnished Crown
Stella Stella	Author	A Widow And A Friend, The South Side Of Heaven
Stephanie Bailey	Author, Love Coach	Dating Like A Football Coach - Finding Your MVP
Tiffany Flowers Towns	Author	I Wish I Had Never
Victoria Anderson	Author	More Than Your Trauma
Valerie Staton	Author	Healthy Living and Stress Management
Victoria Pearson	Author	Embrace Your Voice, The Art Of The Hook
BWA Team		
P. Henson	CEO, Founder	
Denise L.	Design	
Felicia K.	Administrative	
Khoury S.	Te chni cal	
Michelle H.	Education	
Taryn L.	Operations	
Valerie S.	Editing	

BWA
BLACK WOMAN AUTHOR
PAULETTE HENSON